Far/Not Far

J. Warren Lunne

ISBN-13: 978-0-9966900-5-8

What's inside...

For everyone who is fighting cancer
or supporting someone that is…

part 1

Poems of Want

J. Warren Lunne

Far/Not Far 1

Thirty years
A score and a half
Radio silence
Near misses
Pick up the pieces
Each calendar's ashes
Await resurrection
Each unwritten letter
Written in sotto voce
Averse to any intimation
That she could be the one
Humor and modesty
Words emitted for no one
But only for her to hear
Lure of eye contact
Ponder her smile
Summon up the words
Damn, is all you've got
Exchange of music
Playlist foreplay
Far away across a great divide
Where mountains bleed shadows
And cold lonely nights
One foot planted firmly
On the first step of the gallows

J. Warren Lunne

Anchors & Rope

The current whips my face
And my legs, they won't bend
Oxygen deprivation
Only benefits the dead
Suffer and sink
Suffer and climb
Too heavy, this burden
To fall and then rise
Stagger down to the summit
Scale the same mountains
With the same tattered hope
We act like those drowning
Need anchors and rope
Push on to the bottom top
Push to climb that mountain
In the depths of a dark, black sea
Others climbers are blind - just like me
Quick to judge; quick to eviscerate
See the blindness
Where darkness and misery elope
And we all cheer the rescuers
As they toss the drowning
Anchors and rope

Regret

Afternoon siesta
Abnormal delusion of respite
Eyes drift to closure
Sharp knock upon the door

Dress and respond
In my finest pajamas
Contemplate wielding the bat
That I use as a welcome for strange bananas

Two men in black stand on my front porch
"We regret to inform you…" says the first
"Go away," I interrupt him
"I will never understand the risk."

The men fade into the darkness of the dusk
I grip the bat tightly, as I see
A third man standing under a streetlight
Replete with jaundiced illumination

He waits, stares, and never breaks eye contact
Shut the front door and draw the shades
He never speaks and he won't walk away
And I will never have the chance
To listen, ever again

Wheelbarrow

Bent man
Broken wheelbarrow
Pushing emptiness, across
Hot rocks and sand
Anguished ruddy face
Faces down a firing squad
Employed by poverty
No profit in survival
Just a visitor with unpacked bags
Waiting to be released
From the chains

Of awkward silences…

Fabulous

For my friend Lisa, who always called me JoJo...

This flower bloomed for all to see
She never gave up; she refused to yield
She eased our worries with a golden shield

The dew landed in rapture - ablaze with glee
Eyes cut from diamonds, heart made of gold
No way to measure the depth of her soul

Death isn't the end, it just sets us free
Temporary separation from those that we love
Whatever your beliefs
She looks down from above

And all I can see is her smile
As her glow surrounds us
And we are so blessed and fortunate
She was always fabulous

Far/Not Far 2

I hand the woman the note
It's not a poem or song lyrics
Within sixty seconds
Twenty thousand unmarked dollars
If she loves you enough
She'll rob a bank with you

I didn't write the note
We needed clarity, and
She writes in complete sentences
I manned the scissors to extract the letters
From all the glamour magazines
Stacked on the little table by the toilet

Letters pasted in counterpoint
Felony arts and crafts
Though she's annoyed you cut up
The top-ten sex tips article in Cosmo
If she loves you
She'll forgive you

That's how you know for sure
An amusing little litmus test
Love demands so much
I exit the bank through the front door
Hoping she's waiting, with the engine revving
In our black, nondescript muscle car

Passenger door open, there she is
Sunglasses and black lipstick
You look around the street
No alarm, no cops, no gunfire
If she loves you enough
She'll drive your get-away car

Light reflects off storefronts
It's early - the world still craves caffeine
My heart races - our plan is working
When I realize the one certainty of wealth
If she loves you, then
You don't need a goddamn thing

J. Warren Lunne

Hunting

Run
Chase the birds
Scare 'em up into the sky
To their deaths
"Keep going," Dad yells
I pause - hands on hips

Cornhusks whither, already dead
Grey clouds block the sun
Roll across the South Dakota sky
Lifeless, yet animated
Adhering to their fate

Dad and Uncle Larry are out of sight
They want to shoot birds
It's more fun than being home
Mom prefers Dad be out here as well
Our dog Jake died last month

Wasn't much of a bird dog, just a mutt
So I have to run
Scare up the pheasants
It'd be more fun if Jake was here
I'd have someone to talk to at least

Cold air bites my lungs, but
Dad gets mad if I take too long

He says I should pay attention
Hunting is dangerous
People get hurt, killed even

Commotion, flaps, and honks
I see the birds and get low

SHOT! SHOT! SHOT!

My ears ring
The birds survive
Cussing continues
I walk down to where they stand
Dad kicks at the dirt

Uncle Larry laughs and we go back to the truck
We eat sandwiches
Bologna for them
Peanut butter for me
And a Snickers bar

Milk in my thermos
Something else in theirs
After lunch I run the cornrows again
Dad tells me what to do
I do what he says

But he never hits any birds
He sends me back to the truck

The truck is cold and I can see my breath
I push the cigarette lighter in
Warm my hands when its red

Dad and Uncle Blaine come back to the truck
Uncle Blaine carries a bird
Dad's hands are empty
They get in the truck
I sit in the middle to cover up
The burnt hole in the seat

Conversations regarding Mother
On the way home
Mom yelled at Dad this morning
Then scolded me
I just want to stay here
And run by myself down the cornrows

Seven on the Box

Seven on the box!
An order from the darkness
No privacy
No isolation
In Grandpa's house

Bookmark the science fiction
In a house built as an antidote
To the Great Depression
Two bedrooms
One bathroom
Connected by a hallway

TV room and kitchen
Divided by a single seam
Mangy rust-colored carpet

In a horrific collision with
Jaundiced white diamond linoleum

Decay and neglect
Stand watch over this house
Fighting a two-front war
Against hygiene and cleanliness
Not that a teenager worries about such things

Gramps' bed springs whine

As he shifts his weight
I hear his big feet fumble
Scratch the floor
To find his slippers - then silence

There is always a pause
Before any menial function
If you don't pee early, you'll pee outside
That's what my cousin Jessica says

Stuck for the summer with
An decrepit old man
The Lawrence Welk Show
And all the library books you can read

My father is away
Honeymoon number two
Wife number four

My mother is away
In California with a friend
On leave from being a single parent

Time cannot be divided equally
You're given away
Mom and Dad split
Life serves up a sucker punch

Gramps is too idle to die

I'm too young to drive
Too detached to request
The details of his life

When all answers are buried
Sealed safely in their graves
Questions poke through the soil
Nameless people in dusty frames

Only the past can break the silence
Build a stronger fate
Wrapped in family ties and shiny shoes
The mysteries of our elders
Fade to silence at the cemetery gate

Leaving

Mail arrives
Pitch the letters between the coffee stains
On the old panel door
Propped up by milk crates
Power broker desk

Jimmy Bolton scans the mail
Five bills
Three fan letters
An envelope
From the LA County Sheriff's Office

One of the letters
Addressed to Little Jimmy Bolton
A long ago moniker
The long ago hurts
Fan mail first - sometimes they send cash
Not today
No need to open the bills
Or the letter from the Sheriff
He knows what they all say

Growing up as Little Jimmy Bolton
Had its perks
That was the long ago
Never be a kid star
Never get to be a kid

Never know where your parents went
Always know about the debt

A son
Lived somewhere
If he opened the letter from the Sheriff
Maybe he'd learn of
His whereabouts

He often thought of the sage advice
Gary Coleman gave him
It's cheaper to sleep with a hooker
Than a teenybopper who thinks
She loves you
You don't pay hookers to sleep with you
You pay them to leave
After they've slept with you
Fans don't leave

His son's name was Beau
Beau's mom was Kate
Kate was a fan
Fans don't leave
And then you can't get rid of them

Jimmy put on his hat
Nobody recognized him in a hat
Sell the plasma, pay the bills
Maybe he could deliver pizza

Far/Not Far 3

A visitor in the garden
Unsuspicious of the shade
One kiss before love
Is all that she can take

Summer rain, hair in tangles
Dark eyes afire at the stroke of midnight
She refuses an umbrella
Simply out of spite

Hide under an awning
By the Plaza
Or the Met
The past can be outgrown
Eye contact
Touch of hands
Lean into her shoulder

With each new lens
Her features change
Her smile broadens
Brings light to rain

Happiness and anxiety
Breed a subtle despair
Offering up a greedy noose
And an elegant electric chair

Those wounds
Heal slowly
Friends advocate sweetly
Take your time

The visitor in the garden
Makes the roses grow sweeter
The fragrances deeper
You can't unwind
Rush in
Rush forward

Body on body
The last bloom sighs
Candid lovers are the best
On the warmest nights

Blue Line

Wheezy, Chesty, Sweaty
Ms. Ballbricker, Romeo and Julio
Every regular rider
Earns their moniker twice
Theirs and mine

No jets
No limousines
A helicopter is useless
When you live in a studio in Queens

Take the blue line, lumber along
Everybody's body swaying
In unison
Every curb, every pothole
Shifts our frames and figures
One sharp jolt
Bodies shift to the left
Our spines united
In mass transit momentum

Four walls of dialog
Trapped so close to the bone
What are these muthafuckin' people thinking?
I know, honey, I know
Blowjobs aren't cheating, they're just blowjobs
It's your mom, you can't reject her

Human wedge between Romeo and Juliet
A middle-aged woman in a knit cap
It's below freezing
I can see her sweat

The world passes by
Strangers pass by moving windows
Diesel fumes, lovers, crack addicts
All better than television
But a click below Netflix

The unrequited love of my life
"Cindy" with a mole on her cheek
She reads Harry Potter
In the seat by the rear door
I will never talk to her

Can you believe this muthafuckin' shit?

Stairs Down/Elevation Up

Years of service and nary an accolade
At the OK Chemical Company
Employee number five is unhappy
And it's her last day

Hired by the founder, she suffered his heirs
With precious loyalty to a long deceased king
She was a dinosaur, who never bothered
To conquer the fax machine

Much less email or smartphones
She knew too much
She kept the score
For she was the one who buried the bones

In his will, the founder, Owen Knight
Secured Janice's employment until the end of her
life
When he crashed a truck full
Of herbicide and defoliant
She helped him clean and cover it up

Dapper Owen Knight the third
Knows the story and all her intrigue
He fires her anyway - he's busy
Too much to think about

With his fantasy league

So on her last day
When she doesn't give a fuck
She mails select files to the EPA
Then leaves quietly
Because you always take the stairs down
When you rode the elevator up

Runner Three

One to the runner three
Materialistic anarchy
Pavement pounder
Down and outer
Bowing to the monarchy
Crouching low
When bullets fly
Carving up an amber sky
Precisely scripted foreplay
Head to night
Night to day
Head to chest
Back to front
Ride the wave
And seek the crest
Fluorescent day-glo synergy
Thrust a dagger in my breast
And follow one to the runner three

Far/Not Far 4

Asleep
She breathes heavier
Out faster than the light
Ballgame on the radio
Extra innings
Season on the brink
Your arm on pins and needles
Body still, tense
Deserves the rest, she does
One delicious leg coiled around you
As the tenth inning ends
All knotted up
Playoffs matter
No harm in exhalation
Body starved for heat
She pulls you closer
Six more outs
No change
Heart beats faster
Game seven
Third string reliever on the mound
Trying to earn his keep
A pitch and a swing
Centerfield drops back deep
Announcers ask for intervention
Audio mix sublime
The crowd begins to roar

J. Warren Lunne

The game is over
Your love stirs
And mumbles
What's the score?

Drifting

I'm drifting
Sliding away to the midnight life
Higher and higher
No fear or flight
Climb the ladder to get that glider down
I'm thinking
That if there ain't no hell
I'll just wander the streets
I need a trumpet and a slide trombone
Pour me a whiskey-neat
Hey Mr. Drummer!
Hit the snare on the ones and threes
Somewhere in the future
There's a world of peace
Not for me, I'm bitter
But for my nephews and my niece
Got my order in early for the last call in hell
The piano player's grooving
It's his last week here
The woman at the bar calls everyone, "Dear"
We all know the chorus
We just struggle with the last verse
Picked her up for our first date
In a red and purple hearse
She giggled at the moonlight
While we waited on the rain
I could tell her that I love her

J. Warren Lunne

Or I could say it to a stranger
Nothing's left for certain
When every day's the same

Illogical Aspirations

Strut and stride
Along the boulevard
Offer fakers in bronze Mercedes
Two gnarled middle fingers
Raised high
Veteran or hippy
Both?
Pitching rocks
At road signs
Trajectory dimension
Sun on ruddy forehead
No hat
Long hair
Always shorts and hiking boots
Shirt optional in summer
Red grey beard
No sunglasses
You want the fuckers to see
The gleam in your eye
When you show them how you hate
Errant thoughts of life
Gone bad
Dead ends, canceled flights
Atlas couldn't bear
That chip upon your shoulder

J. Warren Lunne

Stay Away From Me

Stay away from me
Stay away from me
I don't want to change
If the world is still asleep
Say a prayer for me
Say a prayer for me
I don't want to die
Staring up from a headstone
To a cloudless amber sky
I've got less to lose
Lose my life for self
Wake when all I know
Is there's nowhere here to rest
Stay here with me
Stay here with me
Every day is just a dream
And time's the enemy
Follow the trail to the end
When you know where
You want to be

Return to Zero

Life's work
Returns to zero
Reset
Leverage rest
Laundry done
Bed unmade
All the clothes
You'll wear again
Folded neatly
From the laundry bin
Watch others clean
Impulsive OCD
Fine dust on lamps
Paintings and pictures
She runs her finger
Through the dirty zones
A test and testament
To neatness
Life in disorder
Preempt vanity
Tasteless and vacant
You can never have all your clothes clean
Unless you wash the last load naked

Far/Not Far 5

Take a lover on an overnight train
Turn on the lights
Flip up the nightshade
Kinetoscope sex
Paint a picture for the landscape
Drive a two-lane blacktop
For a hundred days
Find a diner with a neon jukebox
Collect skipping stones
As you gather your thoughts
Bleed the laughter from a rainy day
Hold em longer when they're faraway
Plant a tree
When you need some shade
Watch old movies
With the sound down low
Read the lips
Watch the dark eyes glow
Climb a mountain
When you've nothing to prove
Be advised - all heat needs fuel
Write your chapters
Submit them to the moon
Wait for the revisions
Throw them away
Life is perfect
When you find the One

Far/Not Far

J. Warren Lunne

part 2

Ribcracka

(When the Coroner Sings the Chorus)

J. Warren Lunne

Bug Stubble

Car Wash
Bug stubble and mud
Baked on a faded white bumper
Idle Mike orders new car scent
Wanders inside
Pays the cashier, Suzie Clu
Who fumbles his change
She makes no effort to retrieve his two cents
"Sorry for the convenience"
Ignores him while she tortures her gum

Should have paid with a card
Blood rushes into his skull
As he picks up the coinage
Systolic kick drum beats time in his brain
Nags him to take his blood pressure meds
He could lose some weight – twenty pounds
Maybe forty-five

Idle ponders competence
Defers to absolution
Steps out onto the patio
Two hours to noon
Mercury at 107
Arizona sun brings the heat
Big bang flashback
Idle shrugs off sunscreen

A burn would add color
If not a little carcinoma
The heat reminds him:
He's hungry for tacos

A book he'll never finish
Open to page ten
The saga of redemption
Starring a feral dog named Oskar
The abused, heartbroken, and neglected
Should all be reincarnated
As a dog lover's dog

Fellow customers sift through virtual lives
Idle reads and his car matriculates
Minimum wage platoon with
Clean rags, strong backs
Student loan debt
Or family south of the border
Tends to spit polish and bug removal
Lost in admiration: For Oskar
The one-eyed bastard love child
Part pit bull, part wolf
Idle doesn't hear the crash

T-Bone Taylor

Collision
Standard bumper-to-bumper sucker puncher
Blue SUV up yellow sedan's ass
Lawyer's bread, butter, and honey
Glass shards
Taillight vomit splatter pattern
Art on the thoroughfare

T-Bone Taylor emerges
From her banana-colored sedan
Snaps a pic
Posts on Instagram
All parental lectures and
Overtures aside
She always texts on her truancy drives
Surveys the glass on the searing asphalt
She was texting, but the SUV hit her
This wasn't her fault

Shock to anger
Ready to blow
Subsiding guilt
Presses record on her new iPhone
Marches towards the SUV
She means business this isn't a game
"Hey mister, you hit me!"
She yells with all of her six-foot-one frame

No movement
Driver slumped, static and still
She slaps the window
His body offers no response
Too soon to think he's a corpse
He sure looks blue and unwell
Door handle: locked
Ire to concern
She hammers a fist against the glass
He stirs not
No change in his status
Too much time has elapsed
She cocks her arm and strikes the window
Slightly off, hits the frame
Her left wrist snaps
"Shit!!!"
Tennis season is over for T-Bone Taylor

Shoeless Jonah

Startled
Idle looks out to the street
Sees a girl hopping
And holding her fractured wrist
Am I witnessing a homicide?
Or just the usual road rage?

Car washing halts
Workers and customers
Stand in repose
A Greek chorus of anxious consternation
Discomfit, and woes

Out in the street
A man might be in danger
This woman might be losing her mind
But there are appointments to keep

A carwash employee dodges traffic
Makes his way to the scene
Idle waxes nostalgic for Frogger
As the strapping young man
With a full and rich tan
Navigates three lanes of traffic
A median
And an irascible jogger
On further review

Idle thinks the man's not dark, but Indian
The kind Columbus set out to find

Traffic drowns the dialogue
Between girl and the Indian
Idle reads the universal body language
Of humanity
The pair's concern is clear

The blonde cradles her fractured ulna
Motions at the SUV with her other elbow
No hesitation
The man punches
One fist through window
Driver's side rear
Second glass vomit splatter pattern

Awkward extraction
Driver out on the ground - unconscious
Idle cannot see the driver's face
Hiking shorts reveal ruddy legs
Feet adorned with nary a shoe or sock

There he is
Shoeless Jonah
Prostrate and unconscious
On the searing asphalt

A pharaoh hound scrambles out

From the back of the SUV
The beast looks around frantically

Sees nothing familiar
Lopes away: graceful, athletic
Crimson tan coat
Glows in the sunshine

The hound and Idle make eye contact
For a moment
Idle sees its head is almost human
The hound has the face of an young woman
Rapt with admiration
For the beauty of this beast
He nearly drops his phone

Samar the Tan

Samar wants none of this
An injured white girl
A dead or dying man
And a loose dog
This is not a winning ticket
He turns back, towards
Onlookers and bystanders
They all avert their gaze
Search for the meaning of life
On their phones

He could have done nothing

He spots Suzie Clu peering out
Watching him from the car wash office
He needs to take charge
Looks to the blonde
"What do we do now?"
She's too busy watching hound
Bound away and out of sight
Her wrist bone pokes through flesh
All color dissipates from her white skin

"Is he dead?"

Samar is not a doctor
He washes cars

Life and death pop quiz
No lecture
No open book
Just…go

The blonde looks down at Shoeless Jonah
Lifeless at his curtain call
"Do CPR. You know how, right?"
"I've seen it on TV shows."
"Give it a shot. Can't hurt."

Samar kneels next to Shoeless Jonah
Feels the heat of the street
Bite through his khakis
Feels for a pulse
Nothing
Places his hands
On Jonah's chest
Pushes down, unsure
Then again
Hard to kill a dead man
Very little risk
Still Samar imagines the girl
Would do better
Even with a broken wrist

J. Warren Lunne

Donna in Dispatch

"9-1-1. What's your emergency?"

Long pause
Caller ID reads: "Mike, Idle"

"9-1-1, What is your emergency?"

Idle relays the events of the day
Car accident on Oracle
Near the car wash
Blonde girl, an Amazon
Indian man performing CPR
On a fellow on the ground

Donna peppers Idle with standard Qs
Who
When
Where
How many

Turn over a terrorist to a dispatcher
You'd learn all you need to know

Idle mentions the dog
Jumped out of the SUV
Ran off
Send a dog catcher

Donna stifles a giggle
An Animal Control Officer is on the way
No such thing as a dog catcher
Unless you count the sickos
Who kidnap animals
For maniacal science experiments

Beautiful dog
Never seen anything like her
One of those Egyptian dogs
Like you see with the fay-rows
Real beaut

Donna in Dispatch
Needs to know
If others are injured
Idle refuses and describes the dog
Medium size with a coat so golden
That dog could move
It could almost fly
There's a deputy pulling up
Do you want me to stay on the line
Rapt by his voice
Donna searches for reasons
Dispatch is short-staffed
There are other emergencies

"No, I'll let you go. Thanks for calling."

Deputy Ribcracka

Lights on
Siren whines
Deputy Ribcracka finally arrives
Love child - John Wayne and Chuck Norris
Steps out of his blazer
Surveys the scene

Relieves the Indian man from CPR
His first compression
Crack-pop-crunch
Shoeless Jonah's chest cavity cartilage
Ribcracka circulates Jonah's vitals
Pumping in time to an AC/DC anthem
Full throttle in his mind

He could have been a drummer
Coulda woulda shoulda
Health insurance and steady paychecks
Got the nod, over
Groupies and discordant sound checks
He's raising a daughter solo
Today, she's on his mind

"Isn't that going to hurt him?"
Asks the Indian

"Gotta be forceful."

Ribcracka responds

Compression pops
He mentally preps
To lecture his daughter
About boys and sex
He looks up at the blonde

"What's your name?"
T-Bone Taylor replies
"Hang in there, Taylor. Help is on the way."

He sizes her up
Slightly older than his daughter
He could use her advice
Life in crisis he understands
Average-everyday
Not blood-and-guts-and-gore
That spooks him to the core

The sound of sirens
Some near and some not so close
"Don't forget about the dog."
Taylor scolds

Wanda Nada, EMT

More lights and siren
Ambulance on the scene
Movement, hustle, and here she is
Wanda Nada, EMT

Into action
No BS
No bravado
Jonah's face rings a bell
Her throat constricts
Too dry to swallow

Ribcracka steps away
Makes room for Nada
Gurney Gary follows
He a cart
And a kit
Flush with electro-medical potpourri
Wanda pumps
Jonah continues dying
She dated this lifeless sod
Long before her hair was thin and grey
Youth and dignity
He stole both
Shoeless Jonah and young women were a thing
His villa on the northwest side
Replete with Middle East antiques

She loved him
He dumped her
She fills in the blanks daily
The in-between
Loss of time
Self worth
No man
No human
Should never touch a heart
It's a sad state of affairs
When a rose
Believes its place is underfoot

Now his life is in her hands
She'd prefer he bake to death
On this pavement
Sometimes we breathe life
Into the dying
Simply so we can finish
Them off with indifference
Wanda cracks Jonah's chest - hard
Ribcracka tells her to ease up

J. Warren Lunne

On the Scene Janeen

It's a fucking wreck!
We don't need a remote!
Screams On the Scene Janeen
Tucson's top investigative newscaster

"Apparently, there's a body."
Says Video Vinnie.
Her cameraman and cohort
He flips a bitch on Oracle
Hits the gas
To get there faster

A dead body is needed
For the twelve o'clock news
Forget the call center corruption
And the CEO crook
Post a lifeless body
On
Twitter
Instagram
And Facebook

Hashtag: endofthefuse

Idle Mike in Drive

Idle ponders
His confab with
Donna in Dispatch
She cared about the dog
He could sense her empathy
Should he call her back
Or let it be

Idle's mantra
Life calls for ignorance
At all times
Just to secure
A peaceful state of mind

Life at the car wash
Trends towards normal
Car ready
He leaves a tip
Drives away
Watches Wanda Nada pump
Nearly runs the newswoman over
She flips him off
He waves - a feeble response

Four blocks from the wash
He slams on the brakes
The book!

Ponders Oskar
Decides to track down the pharaoh hound
Parks along the river walk - The Loop
Joggers, bikers, and runners
All pass by
As he sets out to search
For the beautiful dog

T-Bone Taylor (Teen Advocate)

T-Bone Taylor
Looks around
Pines and hopes
To see that loping hound

On the Scene Janeen
Is soon in her face
Taylor isn't ready for her close-up
No one ever is
And just like that
She's on the news
"Tell me how it happened."
Inquires Janeen

Taylor pauses then lays it all out
She's a star and role model
"Never text and drive."
T-Bone says.
Her mother texts her during the interview
To tell her to stand up straight
On air, she looks at her phone
Straightens up
Commuter trolls drive by
Whistle and holler
"Fuck off!"
She yells and flips the bird
Jane begins her wrap up

With that discouraging word
Taylor grabs the microphone
"There's a beautiful dog out there!"
And relays the events of the crash
Jane wrestles the microphone back
Ties it up
Sends it back to the studio
Taylor looks pallid
Her arm slowly turning blue

Ginger Gryphon

Ginger sits at home
Faithfully watching the news
Collision on Oracle and a body
She sees the yellow SUV
Knows her ex is dead
Traffic will be a bitch
But if those gridlocked drivers
Only knew humanity's gain
Teenage blonde appears onscreen
Speaks of a missing dog
Ginger knows this beast
A canine known as Nefertiti
Spellbound and speechless
She pours another martini
The hounds should be hers
Divorce lawyers can remove
The wanting from the wanted
With staggering finesse
She leaves her condo
In a shuffle of a hurry
Clutches her keys and her purse
No need to wait for sobriety

Suzie Clu

First responders race away
Life resumes
Cars
More car washes
Suzie Clu watches Samar cross the street
Back to the car wash
The manager shakes his hand
Others pat Samar on the back
Suzie isn't clueless because she's dumb
Four credits shy of her college degree
She has kept Samar in the dark
About his future
And hers
The conversation we need to engage in
Is the most likely to put off
She told her best friend
Who told countless others
Now she stands at a cashier counter
Decorated in 90s neo-modern furniture
Surrounded by useless tchotchkes
She wants to be near Samar
She is mad he doesn't know
Less mad that she hasn't told him
She doesn't need a man
She needs a partner
Two customers await Suzie's attention
She pines out the window for Samar

She's convinced herself that he was flirting
With the young blonde girl
She wants to hold Samar
Tell him he's a hero
And then slap him

The Bowman

News travels
While pants are put on
World Wide Web
Casts a long shadow
Misunderstanding
Rumors lead to truth
News story forward
Video: reporter and blonde Amazon
Talking of a car wreck
A broken bone
A beautiful dog
Bowman knows
This is stolen treasure
From a vault
Out on the Rez
The company hid experiments
So many cover-ups
So few records
Hybrid breeding
Man and beast
On the periphery
Woman and beast
Put a stop to the past
Transgressions of science
On the human condition
All tests fail
To prove we are human

He packs his bow and some gear
Into his Chevy
Drives into the night
Maps a route to Tucson

J. Warren Lunne

Intermezzo
(As sung by Coroner Basso)

This man upon my table
He is naked, he is dead
He was shoeless when they wheeled him in
His face was ruddy; his legs were red

Always read your autopsy
Before your flesh goes cold
It's moral wrapped in anomaly
At least that's what I'm told

The smell of death and formaldehyde
There's a murder; here's a suicide
A heart attack and an overdose
We block the reaper but he's always close

And so some pray
While others meditate
But until that day
When proof is fate

Our one-way ticket
Is that little tag upon our toe
Your life may stop tomorrow
Or today, you just never know

First Glass: Red, Second Glass:White

She owes her life to herself
Everything
She wants a few weekends back
Secrets are dignity's armor
She will survive
But first, there must be wine

Home from work
Every step a reprieve
From keeping the world alive
First glass red
Laundry in
Replay the images of injured and dead

Erase emergency responses
Second glass white
Feed the dogs
Broken wrist cleared from sight
Dogs and Wanda
Around the block twice

Third glass red
Pecans for dinner
Fourth glass white
Vomit
Sleep on bathroom floor

Wake up at 3:42 AM
Jonah's dead – a man with a monochrome soul
Remembers all the letters she wrote
While he ignored her
Stable not sober
Running clothes on
Dressed all in black
She leaves the house
Like she's never coming back

Donna Wants To

Donna leaves dispatch
Clutches a cake tray
Food is omnipresent
Shiftwork gastronomy
Police departments
Dispatch centers
Dungeons and platoons
Hours: unnatural
Blue glow of screens
Darkness to dayshift
To nightshift
With life in between
Bad skin
Weight gain
Donna wants out
Idle's contact info on her phone
"Like you see with the fay-rows"
Please over and over
In her head
She loved the sound of his voice
Arrives home
Sets down the cake tray
Runs to the toilet
Ponders calling him
She knows he won't mind
Men rarely mind when women call
From the throne

J. Warren Lunne

She stalks him
Not on Facebook
Nor on Twitter
Idle Mike has no virtual presence
Building this mystery
She readies to call him
And prepares to press send

Gurney Gary

Another return to his modest house
Saved six
Lost one
Shoeless man dying
As they pulled up to the ER
Nothing is odd
When you've seen it all
No time for remorse
Guilt or shame
Part of job

The shoeless stiff on Oracle
Affected Wanda
Normally she has thick skin
Gurney Gary does too
All first responders do
Mostly
Cracks show
He pays it no more thought
Feeds his dog
Microwaves his dinner
Heat and the exchange of atoms
Between container and food

That Indian guy?
What was his name?
He asked too many questions

Hard to run a Q&A
And give CPR
Only death can stop time
Until science proves
Otherwise
Gurney patiently answered
The man's questions
Even though
He wanted to punch him in the mouth

Gary always heard his grandparents
In his mind
They told him that black men
Must never lose their cool
When he was younger
He was a problem child
Always hated school
Somehow he survived
Has a good job
A good job he knows he can't risk
For all the lives he's saved

He hears his grandmother's voice
Ring through his brain
As though it were yesterday
"Stay out of the troubles."
She'd say
"Always stay out of the troubles."
And Gurney Gary always had

Idle in a Hurry

Scours the bike path
Finds nothing
He's not a tracker
Or subtle
Never was and never will be
He just wants to find
This goddamned dog
Beauty
Grace
Poise
The canine had it all
Loping down the street
Horripilation
As he replays the woman's face
On the dog's body
Watching the beast
Transports him through time
Idle never fond of possession
And now a strong feeling inside
Like the pilgrims landing in the New World
He wanted to own the wild
His cellphone rings
He doesn't recognize the number
Ignores the call
A few steps down the trail
Beep notification alerts
To a waiting voicemail

He pauses
Plays the message
"Um, hi, Mike, or Idle. This is Donna."
Long pause.
"I'd like to talk to you about that dog."
Mike presses callback

Ribcracka Defeated

Ribcracka talks to his daughter about sex
She gags on her macchiato
He's sure she knows
More than she lets him think
She knows
She lacks a dance partner
Sun dresses and long legs
It's a daughter's prerogative
To confound her father

He overheard the blonde girl
Talk to her father
About a boyfriend at the U of A
Ribcracka feels the need to respond
Because, well, he's a first responder
He is unaware of the veins bulging
In his neck and forehead
His mind, homicidal
He will maim anyone
Who goes near his daughter

But she's in command today
At home and in the heart
Our supervisors fluctuate

She's a barista on break at a coffeeshop
He stops by on the way home

Shared awkward silence
Parental lucidity
He departs
She calls him Daddy
All is well

Thoughts abound
To the shoeless one
He ran Jonah's criminal history
Small-time hoodlum with a heart of porn

Jonah's estate
Would make a McMansion
Feel useless and insecure
Yet, dying on Oracle
You couldn't have shaken a nickel out of him

T-Bone Taylor (Teenage Detective)

Doctor Lawrence
Sets her arm
Prescribes the necessary pills
Oblivious to anything or anyone
The dog lingers in Taylor's mind
She wants out of the hospital
Wanders outside
An orderly gathers her up
Only child perfection
T-Bone is the only pet
Her parents allow in the house
Wants to text her beau
Her father has her phone
Can't recall his number
No matter
There are other ways to communicate
Arm in cast
Heart in sling
Hunger and nausea interlope and loom
She feigns sleep
Then escapes her hospital room

J. Warren Lunne

Idle & Donna

They find the tracks or so they think
Rillito to Santa Cruz
Up Canada Del Oro
Towards the Catalinas
This dog moves quickly
Idle and Donna don't

Donna is heavy and out of shape
She joined Mike at the parking lot
Near Thornydale
The sun sinks
Clouds sulk over the Catalinas
Rain falls up on high
Races down the slopes
Into the gullies and washes
"Hopefully the dog doesn't bed down."
Idle states
"In the riverbed."
Donna finishes

"You have a great voice"
She replies
She's cute, but
Idle wishes she could keep up
Patience though

Donna will play a larger role in his life

But they're lagging behind the canine
Tempo of his heartbeat: cha-cha-cha

When you realize you've found your partner
There is no more, I am
There is only: we are

Suzie & Samar

"I want to be an EMT."
Says Samar
Clueless perks up
This is the first ambitious statement
Samar has ever made
She imagines not having
To tell her parents the truth
Their grandbaby's father
Will not be a carwash attendant
He will be an EMT
"That would be good."
Suzie replies
"How do you intend to do that?"
"I will get on the internet and find out."
Google is a cure-all
He wishes he had saved the dog
Too late for regret
Clueless pulls him close
"There is something I need to tell you."
"Is it important?"
He says before kissing her forehead
Suzie's eyebrows perk up
"Maybe you should sit down."

Jonah's Compound

Ribcracka wakes
Soaked in a terrible sweat
Provocation
Jonah's death
Daughter's pending libido
Dresses in black
Makes his way to Jonah's house
One light on inside
Quiet
Static
He ponders his next move
Can't walk to the door
He's here on his own
Not just unethical but flat out stupid
Totally against policy
Everything he believes in
Curiosity tells him to go inside
Instinct tells him to walk away
He shouldn't be here
He flips a bitch (his daughter's term)
Makes his way back past Jonah's compound
A black truck drives towards him
Pulls over and parks in the distance
Ribcracka continues along
He passes the truck and sneaks a glance
Wanda Nada, EMT
He almost brakes

She shouldn't be here
He shouldn't be here
Momentary lapse of ethics over
He hits the gas and drives away
"Get out of my mind."
He says out loud
Hoping Shoeless Jonah can hear him
The dead we fail to save wear our grace
We remain their slaves
He can feel the dead man's chest
In his hands as plain as day
He turns off Jonah's street
Sees an age-raddled blue Chevy
Pays it no mind
Doesn't see Taylor toting an IV bag
Not far behind
Ribcracka leaves
Drives home
Windshield wipers
Beating in time

(Innocent?) Bystanders

Parked outside Jonah's house
Wanda sits
Unsure of the light
On inside
She sees movement
Tracks shadows
Lights on
Lights off
Working a path through the house
A blur whips past her
Wearing a hospital gown
It's T-Bone Taylor
Arm in a cast
Carries an IV
Up to the door
Brazenly rings the bell
A pause and all lights go dark
Wanda follows T-Bone
T-Bone turns towards her, alarmed
"Who are you?"
Wanda stops: no answer
Familiarity
The front door creaks open
Both women stiffen
Out on the porch
Steps Ginger Gryphon
.38 in one hand

Glass of whiskey in the other
"Where the hell is my dog?"
Ginger says
High on painkillers
T-Bone begins crying
"Tell me where my fucking dog is!"
A whistling sound
Like a slight breeze of wind
An arrow through Ginger's forehead
Fires one shot into T-Bone
Before dropping dead
Taylor slumps to the ground
Her wound is fatal
Wanda Nada, EMT
Catches Taylor and sinks to her knee
Before another arrow, enters
The base of her skull
Lights out
For all
And all for nought

Animal Control

Lucinda Russell parked her van
In front of a modest house
She rents, unashamed
Long day
Cats and rattlesnakes
Javelina and rabid skunks
On her way home
She nearly hit
The most beautiful dog
The dog walked up to her
Knelt at her feet
A show of obedience
Lucinda had never seen
Dog's tongue extended
No collar
No tags
Animal shelters need more dogs
Like single mothers need
Deadbeat dads
And Lucinda already has
One of those
Lucinda keeps the dog
It's against policy
But the golden sheen
Has her attention
Home, she leads the hound into the house
Surprises her daughter, Roquelle

J. Warren Lunne

Together, they feed the creature
The hounds rests her head in Roquelle's lap
She names the dog Nefertiti
The dog cocks her head
Upon hearing the name
As though she had
Just been summoned from the dead

When the Coroner Sings the Chorus

When coroner Basso sings the chorus
He sings it all alone
A simple melody played straight through
As your flesh peels away from bone

We are only here or hereafter
Ol' Rigor Mortis hates the laughter
Ol' Riggy, change it up, let me be
Expose the system with harmony

Just another drummer out of time
Discord and cymbal crash
Fall back in line
Kick that bass drum
Make it crash

Three bodies
Two arrows
And a fatal gunshot
No leads
To go anywhere
The rumors are all off base
Deputy Ribcracka on the scene
This is his case

Those who chose love
Woke to live another day

J. Warren Lunne

Chase that beauty (if you must)
Find your faith, you're only dust
We like to think we choose our fate
But the moral is: it chooses us

part 3

Haiku de Bushrod

J. Warren Lunne

Renegade glamour
One damp world of petrichor
Silence the compass

Ethereal saints
Ponder air and water's bite
On a poor stone's soul

Intrepid heart
Soars to insatiable heights
Forgets gravity

Susurration: her
Riparian leisure: lust
Epiphany: him

Wise, demure oak tree
Gnarled spirit full of jest
Climb high and wonder

Enter the ring, tame all
An iridescent mismatch
Rodeo clown truth

Harmonic whisper
The trees content in chorus
Listen with your eyes

Clarion kindness
Tree branches bestow on me
Shade of late July

Exigent desire
Traveling tree canopy
Fleeting lover: light

Timid aurora
Libation to the living
Immured in heaven

Tall mountains: sisters
Draped in fog and formal wear
No mystery dies

Sunrise amulet
Take the safety off this life
Always share halos

Tall somber trees sway
Leaves shimmer in frosted light
Hope and heat: equals

Skipping stone ripple
Cuts across an azure sky
Reflecting distance

Rainbow contraband
Spectrum riddle writ on high
All eyes held hostage

Lucid River: race
Gravity flows across time
Space deals no mercy

Horizon falls trace
Branded sky salutations
Earth relents gently

Granite companion
Stone too tender to crumble
Coarse to smooth: in time

Thoughtful pantomime
Birds cling to narrow branches
All hearts seek shelter

No moon to eclipse
Sovereign hearts on display
Solar love all night

Nascent rhythm speaks
Beats tempo to the punch – crash!
Pendulum hips rise

Derelict seasons
Overlap in their beds, blankets
Frost breath silver

No road ended here
Hearts jumped the track, landed long
All landings haunt us

Back to back silence
Race over the dunes, wonder
Why the ocean left...

Roots commingle time
Fingers, trees, and ears all ring
Stay here forever

Shadows share nothing
Lest Earth is not for dreamers
Stand behind no one

To find your silence
Hold a familiar book close
Feel hearts intertwine

Dewdrop outlaws weep
In heartless syncopation
Holsters and roses

Far/not far: one stone
One throw, two skips, three ripples
Skim float dip fly rise

Trailhead destiny
Hearts found in elevation
Kindness with each step

Rivers never cease
Travel, spread life, join the sea
Never judge raindrops

Birds in air: segue
Flight certain: joy probable
Rich souls stew over soup

Spirit: strong and true
The end of the trail: never
Tail Wagger the Great

Hard to the finish
A river that never slows
Fighter: strong and true

A blossom strong rose
Sweet color glows in the mist
Resist her smile? No

Mountain to mountain
Left to admire the distance
Marked by the valley

Mysterious eyes
Smile so sweet - radiant heat
Spirit: calm and wild

Radiant flowers
Solid roots: kindred giggles
This rose knows the way

A soul full of grace
Shape, space, and time: unity
Hearts were made to dance

Tame the river brave
Sail to the horizon, your
Future in plain view

Quick old granite cliffs
Run slower than the trees they shade
Climb them both, listen

J. Warren Lunne is an award-winning filmmaker. He has been employed as a lifeguard, dishwasher, playback operator, dude ranch chore man, post production supervisor, associate producer, artist-in-residence at an alternative high school, public access manager, and public information officer.

www.joelunne.com

www.ingramcontent.com/pod-product-compliance
Lightning Source LLC
Chambersburg PA
CBHW062010040426
42447CB00010B/1992